EBURY PRESS

WARMTH

One of the most popular writers on Instagram, Rithvik's words have never failed to comfort his readers. His words feel like home and refuse to leave your heart. *Warmth*, his first book, was published in 2021, and it was very well received. His book, *I Don't Love You Anymore*, which was published in 2024, became a national bestseller. Rithvik lives a simple life and wants to inspire people to hold on to hope and love themselves more. You can connect with him on Instagram: @wordsofrithvik.

ALSO BY THE SAME AUTHOR

I Don't Love You Anymore

Warmth

words for anyone
trying to move on

RITHVIK SINGH

EBURY
PRESS

An imprint of Penguin Random House

EBURY PRESS

Ebury Press is an imprint of the Penguin Random House group of companies
whose addresses can be found at global.penguinrandomhouse.com

Published by Penguin Random House India Pvt. Ltd
4th Floor, Capital Tower 1, MG Road,
Gurugram 122 002, Haryana, India

Published in Ebury Press by Penguin Random House India 2024

10 9 8 7 6 5 4 3 2 1

ISBN 9780143469520

Typeset in Adobe Garamond Pro by MAP Systems, Bengaluru, India

www.penguin.co.in

For my mother,
who carries skies
in her eyes
and wears grace
like flowers in her hair.

POETRY AND PROSE ABOUT

loving
learning
leaving
hoping
hurting
healing
believing
building
blooming

in no specific order

My words will feel like home to you.

It's been raining
ever since you left,
and here I am,
making paper boats
of your memories,
slowly trying to
let go of you.

A lover found their moon today
and a dreamer kissed the sky.
A flower blossomed today
and a caterpillar finally
became a butterfly.
A heart was touched
by the sun today after years
and the wind danced in joy.

But it's okay if nothing great
happened to you today.
It's okay if you're yet to find
what your heart deserves.
It's okay, for I know,
and you must know it too,
that one day, you'll bloom,
and it's totally okay
if today wasn't that day.

—*hold on to hope*

Sunflowers cannot stay alive
in the absence of the sun,
but you're not a flower,
and you can always
choose to bloom,
with or without someone.

Hopeful hearts are full of life, but sometimes they feel lifeless, too. People who shine brightly on most days sometimes get lost in the darkness, and birds who love the sky sometimes fall to the ground. But you must know that hopeful hearts keep holding on to hope, people discover the sun within themselves, and brave birds dare to fly again.

—*don't give up*

Even rain can't fall
as gracefully as humans
do when in love.

Flowers are waiting
for spring to arrive
and just like them,
I'm waiting for autumn
to leave my heart.

It's the things that are
left unsaid that take up
the most space
in our hearts.

But why do you love them with your whole heart,
the people who leave you feeling empty?

Honeybees give nothing
to flowers but drain them;
sunflowers give nothing
to the sun but feed on its light.
Sometimes, people do the same to you.

Bury your fears
before they reduce you
to a bird with broken wings.

Allow your heart
to fall over and over again
until it's finally ready to fly.

And you'll soon find yourself
far away from all apprehensions
and closer to your dreams.
Flowers will grow
where you had
buried your fears
and the sun will smile back.

—*bury fears, not dreams*

Perhaps when you spend all your time loving someone's dark, you slowly start forgetting about the light that lives in your heart.

And maybe, all we want is to be loved on days when there's a wildfire inside us and no flowers are blooming. When there are no stars in the night sky and the moon refuses to shine. When life isn't kind to us and nothing seems fine. Maybe all we want is someone who stays with us even on our darkest days, and maybe that person is the only one who truly deserves our light.

Some people feel like
sunsets and rainbows.
With a handful of light
in their arms,
they plant hope in
every heart they touch.

It's almost magical, you see,
when you fill
someone's heart with love,
your own heart feels full.

You're so much more than
what people
see in you—
you're a home to hope,
strong enough
to work on your weaknesses;
you fall like rain
and rise like a storm.

And it's okay
if people fail to see
the strength with which
you hold yourself together
even on days when you're vulnerable.

It's okay if people
cannot understand your heart,
for not everyone can fathom
the depths of an ocean;
a thousand people
can *know* someone,
but only a handful
can *understand* them.

But may you never forget
you're much more

than someone's opinion of you,
you're much more
than what people around you
are capable of seeing in you.

If looking into their eyes
makes you smile like never before,
accept that your heart has finally
found itself a home.

One day, you just find someone who fills your heart with the fragrance of a thousand flowers. Someone who ends the wars you've been fighting against yourself. Someone who makes you realize why poets write about love and why people still believe in the magic of letting someone enter their souls.

Time doesn't stop, only people do.
Love doesn't leave, only lovers do.

Some sunsets bring back old memories,
others help us make new ones.

I hope you find someone
who fills your heart
with so much love
that it doesn't
feel heavy any more.

Sunsets and self-love will save your soul.

You look at me in a way that makes my heart melt the way snow does when the sun kisses it, the way lovers do when they watch the sunset together. Your words are a reflection of the warmth you carry inside you. This heart was a graveyard, and you, you with your love, made every ounce of it smile for the first time after decades of pain. It's strange how someone can make you feel a zillion emotions all at once. It's strange how someone's mere presence can make you feel so safe, vulnerable and strong, all at once. You are the breath to the feelings I thought I wasn't capable of handling any more. Your eyes constantly tell me you're in love with me, and my heart never gets tired of saying it feels the same way for you.

—*you make me bloom*

You'll meet many people
who would promise
to gift you the stars,
but I hope you
wait for the person
who would make you
shine like one.

Listen to people
for they may be dying
to tell someone
how they're feeling.

—*and the same goes for your own heart*

I wonder as I look outside the window,
trapped in the love of morning rain
the trees seem to be patiently waiting for sunshine,
the same way I've been waiting for you.

Busy grieving the person
who left you in chaos,
you forget to appreciate
the one who saved you from it.

Hold a cold heart
with love and watch
how it transforms into a flower.

Love is an ocean
that reminds people
of the depths
of their own hearts.

Some people are feelings
which refuse to leave the heart.

You love flowers even when it isn't spring.
May you learn to love yourself the same way.

So take a deep breath and let them go,
for they don't deserve the right to stay in your life,
the ones who do not understand your soul.

Today, I forgive myself,
not for loving you too deeply
but for failing to love myself
the same way.

Love your growth
for there are people
who spend their entire lives
with their feet and eyes
on the ground.

Love is a bird that gifts wings to every heart it touches.

It's okay to not
be enveloped by rainbows, my friend,
until you can feel
the warmth of sunshine
around you.

Happiness isn't about places,
it's about people who feel like home.

I saw the moon,
gently looking towards
the earth—
smiling on seeing
lovers holding hands,
watching shooting stars,
falling in love with the
darkness of the night
while promising to be
each other's light.

I believe in love,
but my heart doesn't
believe in the people
who claim to understand it.

So every time someone
tried to get closer to me
I pushed them away.
I didn't care to see
the love in their eyes,
but only impending heartache;
almost as if falling in love
would reduce my heart
to a barren autumn tree,

longing for a spring
that may never arrive.
I kept running away from love,
trying to save my heart
from the eventual pain,
but then one day,
I ran into you,
and the warmth that I was
frightened would burn me
caressed my heart
and wrapped me in its embrace.

That's when I realized
you cannot run away
from what awaits you
and love doesn't always
lead to heartbreak—
sometimes, love stays
and it's worth the risk.

I remember every little detail
that I so want to forget.
I wish to let go of your memories
but also hold on to them,
and that's the ugliest state
one's heart can be in.

There are times when I look at you and feel you're no longer the person you used to be. But then I look at myself, and I wonder if you think I've changed a lot too. I no longer send you pictures of flowers or ask if we can watch a sappy movie together. You no longer tell me about your cooking nightmares, and I no longer ask. These days, we smile a lot less when we're next to each other, and there is much more silence than there ever was. Perhaps that's what time does—it changes things. You think your love for someone will remain unchanged even if everything else doesn't stay the same, but unfortunately, it changes too. Sometimes, in ways you don't like. Sometimes, in ways you had never imagined. And only silence and memories are left where there was love once.

Solitude doesn't scare me. Silence does.

Some people make a home
in your heart
and promise to stay with you
even if the world was ending,
and your innocent heart forgets
how so many people
make so many promises
to so many people
every single day,
but not everyone cares enough
to keep the promises they make.

It's only a matter of time
before you realize,
you're going to lose them,
but you never accept that
you never really had them.

People don't leave your life
all at once—
they leave your life
little by little,
moment by moment.
And it takes years before you
finally realize you were

just a part of their vacation—
a tiny part of their rainbow-filled days,
and never really a part of their life.

Don't let such temporary people
enter your heart,
for they would
ultimately leave you alone,
with your only companion
being the painful memories
of the time you spent loving them,
only to be left heartbroken in the end.

I've loved you in silence for so long,
my heart doesn't know
how to express itself any more.

How I felt like when you left:
- – A leafless tree in a spring-kissed forest
- – A withered flower in a bouquet
- – A playlist full of sad songs
- – A letter too drenched in the rain to be read
- – A prayer made with an empty heart
- – An empty house
- – A poem without a rhyme
- – A loud war
- – Silence

There can be light
all around you
and inside you,
and you can still feel
lost in darkness.

I know you listen to the same song whenever you're sad. I have your favourite lyrics tattooed on my heart. Whenever you're upset, don't think twice before falling into my arms.

But people aren't flowers
and you shouldn't break them
just because you find them beautiful.

Jealousy consumes your heart,
says my mother,
and gives birth to a version of you
that leads you to self-destruction.

The memories that live inside you
can either give you a reason to live
or turn you into a graveyard.

I remember how you were wearing a shirt the colour of the sky the first time we met. You told me you loved music, and I asked you to send me a few songs you love, and you didn't reply. You had an ocean voice, the kind that can make anyone fall in love. With time, I lost count of the number of sunsets we watched together. I no longer remember the number of times I asked you which song you were humming and you refused to tell me. But I do remember how the day before the sky took you away, you gave me your playlist and sang me a song, and I bit my lips and whispered, 'Stay.' Life left you too soon. You were the music of my life, and there has only been silence ever since you left. We're not in the world any more. And although this distance doesn't make me love you less, it breaks my heart nonetheless.

If your heart is aching, tell it everything that person failed to tell you. Make it feel loved. Be there for yourself and remind yourself that your healing should matter to you more than whether or not you matter to someone else.

The only thing that I could hear when you were next to me was the sound of our hearts coming together to create magnificent music. There's silence now where there was music once. But the tragedy is that even in the silence, I can hear my heart breaking.

Don't make your home
in someone who is foreign
to their own feelings.

But have you seen how your eyes shine, my love?
The sun melts for people like you.

Some days,
I'm so full of light
that I share it with every
person I come across,
but on other days,
I'm just a city
destroyed by floods
hopelessly waiting
for someone to share
their light with me.

—*people need people*

The flowers in your chest
need the warmth
of your own love
to bloom.

You must understand
there's no point
in holding on to someone
when your heart has already
given up on them.

You keep yourself from speaking your heart out when you know your words can break someone else's heart. And when that person is someone you once loved with all your heart, silence is the only option. That's why you fear telling someone when you're falling out of love with them. You get used to their presence, and you don't know how your heart will react to their absence. You want to save their heart and also figure out what your own heart wants. So you keep holding on to them, and you keep burying your feelings. You don't want to break their heart, and you hopelessly wait for them to realize how you feel on their own.

—*matters of the heart*

Sometimes when you tell me that you love me, my heart tells me otherwise.

The world keeps
trying to pull you down
and here you are,
making love with the sky.

Live so wholeheartedly
that when death
kisses your soul,
your spirit dances
in contentment
and does not cry in pain.

Let your heart be your guide,
for it knows who will
leave you alone in the storm,
and who will dance with you in the rain.

There's bravery in choosing not to hurt others.

It's hard to believe in love and harder to believe in the people who say they love you. It's not love if you don't lay your heart bare in front of someone. Doing that requires trust, and I fail to trust people easily. For people don't mean most of the things they say. They say they love flowers but pluck them. They promise to stay forever but walk away easily. They're too fickle-minded to keep promises and too forgetful to remember how to take care of someone's heart. So, I do not think you should blame me for finding it hard to trust others; blame the world for lacking what it takes to love someone genuinely.

I heard the ocean
saying to the sky today,
it is envious of the depths
of the human heart.

Had the ones
with kind hearts
ruled the world,
there would've been
no borders,
only boundless love.

Leaving has never come easily to me. I've always been the person who walks away but never really lets go. The person who saves old movie tickets from first dates and greeting cards from birthdays, who makes a diary entry at night every time someone makes him feel loved. I think this is what happens when you love someone with your whole heart, you just can't get yourself to say goodbye.

I wish to run away from these feelings, but they are determined to stay in my heart. I hate how I feel when I'm next to you. For my heart knows you're here to start a war inside me, and I've lived a serene life for so long that I don't wish to let chaos build a home inside me. You will break my heart, I know, and I hate how my heart still wishes to be with you, how it waits for you every single day and wants me to tell you how much it loves you.

A lover's heart is a flower that
survives wildfires with grace,
and dances fearlessly amidst storms.

There's nothing more poetic than our hearts conversing in moments of shared silence.

Some days
you're the rain that
brings flowers to life.

Some days
you're the hurricane that
makes the sky fall to its knees.

But on all days,
you're equally glorious.
On all days,
you're breathtakingly powerful.

I wanted to run away from you, but you could hear the thoughts running through my head. You'd tell me that you're here to stay without me asking you to say it. That's when I knew you were different. I didn't have to wake up in the middle of the night, praying you were still next to me. I would always wake up to find my hands entwined in yours.

Allow your heart to leave the ones
who cannot fathom its depths.

I carry rivers in my eyes,
mere pain cannot drown me.

My heart finds solace
in the arms of fire,
hatred cannot burn me.

Storms live inside me,
your thunder cannot scare me.

When you told me that you hate being in love, I knew it was grief talking.

If you ask me what is love,
I would tell you about someone
who simply refuses
to leave my heart—
someone who carries
galaxies in their irises,
peace in their arms,
and the ocean in their voice;
someone who feels
like a cold breeze in a desert;
someone whose touch feels like
the kiss of spring to a lifeless tree.

—*love isn't a feeling; it's a person*

Some people
live oceans away from us
but they still feel like home.

You gifted me flowers,
but my heart is only for the one
with whom I can plant gardens.

It's all a facade until you
find that one person who
loves you the way
the moon loves the stars,
the bird loves her freedom
and the rain loves her flowers.

You don't return and recover from your first heartbreak. The first time someone takes your heart in their hands, you feel the safest you've ever felt, only to watch them break it into pieces and leave. It kills the version of you that believes love is uncomplicated. The good part is that it's no longer easy for people to break your heart.

Be mindful of whom you help—
some people don't want
to learn how to fly,
they simply wish
to cut off your wings.

To have someone
who isn't envious
of your potential,
but appreciative of it,
is a blessing.

You keep lying to yourself until your heart is finally ready to accept the truth.

I buried my feelings
in the ground
and no flower has
blossomed ever since.

It's beautifully tragic
how the rain brings back
the happiest and the saddest memories
all at the same time.

You say you're here to save me from the storm, but I think you're the storm I need to save this heart from. You promise to keep me safe, and that scares me, for I've been a lone wolf all my life—bleeding and bruising; but always believing that I don't need anyone else to save me. And the doors of my heart are closed for anyone who makes me feel like I need them to protect myself.

—I'm enough for myself

There are some people you'll date only because they're conventionally prettier than someone who refused to love you. And you'll regret it, because appearances aren't hearts, and if we could fill voids and fall out of love that easily, there'd be no broken hearts in the world. Please don't be with someone you don't love. Please don't break other people's hearts.

They ask me if I've forgotten you. If I've started looking at the sky and smiling again. If tears don't roll down my eyes every time I meet someone who has the same name as yours. If festivals have started feeling like festivals to me again. If spring is finally a season that even I can feel inside my heart. And I pause and then tell them I've not forgotten you, but yes, with time, everything hurts a little less. Perhaps I will never love the sky the way I used to, but I don't hate looking at it any more. A shiver still runs down my spine every time someone calls your name, but I have accepted that you're not going to come back. It's been forever since I last listened to my favorite song or ate my favorite dish, but hey, I'm moving on, slowly, at my own pace. I don't think I will ever forget you, for nobody can ever forget someone they have loved with their whole heart. But I am convinced that we don't forget people. We just get better at not thinking about them. And in time, I will master the art of not thinking about you too.

You will meet people who will fill your heart with hope, only to leave you empty. They will promise to protect your heart, but will end up breaking it. They will promise to make you believe in love again and will leave the moment you decide to give your heart to them. If you meet someone who makes countless promises but fails to keep any, who says they love you, but it doesn't show in their eyes and actions, who promises you the world but does nothing to bring a smile to your face, I hope you choose to walk away from them and save your heart before they break it.

This heart has been painting skies for someone who wishes to stop me from flying.

You break your own heart
by chasing someone
who would never choose you.

There are pieces of my heart breathing in places and people who no longer remember me.

There's this loud silence
that sits between us,
sometimes it's breathtakingly beautiful,
sometimes it's heartbreakingly painful.

Anxiety is an alarm blaring inside your head, and there's no way to snooze it. Your mind turns into a battlefield, and you're fighting against yourself. You constantly worry about the most trivial things and helplessly watch yourself falling apart. There's a storm inside you that just won't get silenced. So when someone tells me to stop being anxious, as much as I want to say to them I'm not anxious by choice, I smile and leave. But I hope the next time someone tells you they're not feeling okay, that they're depressed or anxious or simply upset, listen to them. Listen to them as they speak of their pain and tell you what's been bothering them. Don't tell them what to do. Don't ask them to stay strong. Don't tell them about the time when you felt the same way. Just listen. Listen as they talk about the mountains they've been carrying on their shoulders. Listen as they tell you why their heart is feeling heavy. For sometimes, we don't need profound advice. Sometimes we don't need someone to fight for us or save us. Sometimes we simply need someone to whom we can pour our hearts out without having to think twice. Sometimes we just need someone who would lend us their ears without passing any judgments. Be that person for someone.

There are some feelings that leave you feeling lonelier than ever. I see you with someone else and I don't feel angry. I don't feel upset. But I just can't move. My feet freeze and my heart starts racing. Anxiety grabs me by the throat and refuses to let go until you leave the scene. You make me feel more anxious than you ever made me feel loved. And I hate what your presence does to me.

Some people,
when they
leave your hand,
your heart sinks.

I wanted you to stay so desperately,
that I ended up pushing you away.

I'm scared of calling my friends and telling them that I'm still not over that person. That despite all the hurt they've caused me, it aches my heart to know they're no longer in my life. That despite knowing that their presence makes me anxious, I cannot help but think about them. I'm scared of telling my friends that I still have feelings for someone who didn't think twice before hurting my feelings and breaking my heart. The people who love me are here to comfort me, I know, but how do I tell them that I once again miss the same person, the person who has given me nothing but pain? How do I tell them that I hate myself for feeling this way? They've spent months trying to help me get over that person. How do I tell them I'm still there, 5 p.m., 14 January, outside the cafe where we first met? I'm still there, glued to the past, listening to the only person I've ever loved with my whole heart tell me that they don't love me any more.

People find it easier to leave when they get to know my heart. When I finally put my walls down. So, I try to be more like the people I'm in love with. I won't tell you that I despise your taste in music, and I haven't even watched the movies I'm claiming to love to impress you. *You see, people have never loved me for who I am, so I'll try to be who they want me to be instead.* I'm afraid I'll always pretend to love the things I don't, only so that someone else continues loving me.

It's strange how someone who does nothing for you can mean so much to you. You give your heart to heartless people and romanticize the pain that they bring with themselves. You lose yourself in the eyes of someone who doesn't care to read your eyes. You love them despite knowing they do not value your feelings. You keep forgetting that you don't deserve someone who makes you feel unworthy of love. You risk it all for them and watch your heart drowning day by day while trying to make them fall in love with you.

My heart always knew
you wouldn't stay,
it was me being foolish
hoping my love
could change your mind.

There will be days when your manager will make you feel like you're not worth it. You'll mess up important reports. You'll not get a seat in the metro. Your favorite coffee shop will be closed unexpectedly. Your bank transactions won't go through because of some technical errors. You'll be stuck in traffic for longer than usual. On such days, if you've got a hand to hold and someone who understands your heart enough to give you a hug bigger than all these problems and inconveniences, you're more blessed than you think. On days when nothing makes sense, love makes us feel a little better. Chaos cannot take over when there's someone around you loving you through it all. And if you're currently stuck in chaos with nobody to hold your hand and heart, you're not alone. Your person is out there, somewhere, waiting to make a home out of your heart. Be patient with yourself until you find them, okay?

I thought you would stop me from leaving,
I turned back, but you were already gone.

After You Left:

Day 1: A gentle breeze brushes past my skin, and I'm reminded of you. I look around with restless eyes to find you but to no avail.

Day 5: I'm in literature class. The professor discusses something about Virginia Woolf. I'm reminded of how you used to sit in classes—ankles crossed and left elbow on the table—and how you used to scribble tiny poems at the back of your notebooks.

Day 10: I pass dusty streets and bustling bazaars and tears roll down my eyes like rainfall from a monsoon cloud. I kick a little stone and watch it hop ahead of me.

Day 15: I delete all our messages and snapshots. Memories are all that I'm left with now. I watch the sunset alone.

Day 20: I feel the skies are collapsing and realize it's just my heart.

Day 23: I look at the uneven banks of snow lining the sidewalks. I decide to visit you.

Day 24: I take a few snowdrop flowers and decide to sing you a song. The graveyard feels like home now.

You keep breaking my heart,
but I still call you my home;
you keep lying to me
but I still believe in you;
you never apologize,
but I still keep giving myself
reasons to forgive you.

You can give your heart
to someone
but it's their choice
to either hold it gently
or break it into pieces.

People say pain comes with an expiry date, but sometimes, pain forgets it was supposed to be a visitor. Sometimes, it stays. You forget what your days were like before pain built its home inside you. You look for healing in all the places and people around you, but it is nowhere to be found. And no matter how hard you try to let go of it, it simply refuses to leave your heart.

Your memories embrace my heart and slowly start eating it up.

I hold you close to myself, but I think you're not mine. You move your fingers through my hair and whisper promises of love in my ears, but I think you will be gone by sunrise. It's scary how deeply this heart of mine is scared of being in love. It scares me how I wish to hold on to you. You say you've been a bird all your life, and I'm the only sky that feels like home to you, but how do I believe you? Maybe you do love me. Perhaps you are here to stay. But how do I tell you I'm not ready to be left heartbroken again? How do I tell you I'm not ready to give love another chance? And tell me, how do I save my heart without breaking yours?

—*I'm scared of being in love*

You say you can heal me,
but how do I tell you
that I'm just a flower that
has been plucked
and crushed
and broken apart,
petal by petal
and how can you
heal something
that has already died?

It's sad how we keep searching
for light in the same person
who had left us alone in the dark.

Love isn't something that can be planted in your heart against your heart's will. Love is something that flows like a stream, and you get submerged in it much before you become aware of its presence. You'll be heartbroken, and you will break hearts too, and I hope you know that denying someone's love doesn't make you heartless. People are allowed to tell you they have feelings for you, and you're allowed to feel the way you do. Love isn't always reciprocated, and that's okay. Just because someone doesn't feel the same way about you doesn't make you any less worthy of love. And just because the other person doesn't love you back doesn't mean they're a terrible person. Love is to be shared, not forced or begged for, and that's something most of us learn the hard way.

We could've been a revolution, but you gave up on us, too soon.

You are sad because
your heart still belongs
to someone who no longer
belongs with you.

You deserve someone
who knows what you love,
and loves who you are.

My heart has been
a lost wanderer
ever since you left,
searching for lost memories
between lines of poems,
in yellowed pages of books
and empty cafes,
hopelessly hoping to
hear your voice,
run towards you
and fall into your arms again.

I know there are storms inside you, and you can feel them ripping you apart, little by little. I see the sky is shrouded in darkness right now, and you feel like the sun will never rise again. I know that nothing seems to be going right but please, please believe that this darkness is only temporary. Sunshine will reach you, and the colours of the rainbow will embrace your sky soon. So hold on, keep moving ahead, and don't let your heart give up.

—*persevere*

You're not scared of feeling loved again. You're scared of having to bury your feelings again eventually. You write love poems in your journal and tear the papers off. As if running away from love has ever worked for anyone. As if love requires an invitation or an entry pass to make a home out of you. Be open to love, my love. Not everyone will break your heart.

May you never punish yourself
for someone else's inability
to see the love in your heart.

We have eyes full of stories
and hearts full of memories.

Sometimes, you need to say
goodbye to some people
to say hello to your happiness.

Mourn until you master the art of being happy without them.

You will fall in love with two types of people:

- – Someone who will decorate your sky with stars.
- – Someone who will teach you how to shine alone.

Only the ones with a good heart deserve to enter your soul.

You build walls around your heart and refuse to let anyone build their home inside you. But in your heart of hearts, you want the walls to be reduced to dust. You want someone to break them all, gently, little by little, with love. You want to wear your heart on your sleeves and fall in love again. And perhaps what they say is right—the ones who claim to be afraid of love are also the ones who love the deepest.

It rained all night the day you died. Flowers wilted and birds stopped singing. Trees let go of their leaves despite it being the season of spring. Every fallen leaf sang a sad song mourning your loss. The winds say your death brought autumn to uncountable hearts and made every soul forget what spring feels like. So many autumns have passed ever since you left. The scent of emptiness swirls all around me like an autumn breeze, and grief blossoms on the plant of my life like wildflowers. You rest in the coffin near the parish, and I live in the coffin called life.

—*rest in peace*

We spend our nights thinking about the people who've forgotten us, remembering places that no longer remember us and shedding tears for someone who's still not sure if we really care about them. It's tragic how we spend our days doing the same things we had promised ourselves not to do. It's sad how we care so much about the ones who couldn't care less about us.

You mustn't hold on to
something that only hurts you;
be it people, be it memories.

Our stories and struggles are different,
but we all deserve to bloom.

I hope your days
start with slow songs
and soft kisses,
pancakes that taste
like heaven
and conversations
that diffuse so much
love in the air,
it suffocates sadness
to death.

I hope your nights
are spent in silence,
but never the kind
that rips your heart apart.

I hope life blasts
happy songs around you
until you finally believe
you deserve to be happy too.

I hope your days
start and end with kisses
and you once again
feel that feeling
that your heart
so fondly misses.

You don't have to be
the silver lining for someone
who put you through storms.

Love isn't supposed to burn you,
it's supposed to make you shine.

You're a forgotten library that holds more secrets than one can imagine. Faith in an atheist's house. Poetry that isn't written for everyone. You demand being understood, but it's almost impossible to understand you. You're the words that never make it to the final draft because the world cannot bear so much truth. You're lost memories full of hope. It's a shame that the world has convinced you to believe you aren't beautiful just because you're nothing like the filth of this world.

Even if nobody is there for you on days when you don't feel okay, I hope you choose to treat yourself with kindness and be there for yourself. I hope you listen to your favorite song, take a nap, cry if you feel like and go out for a walk. I hope you don't let a few bad days convince you to believe that you don't deserve happiness. I hope you save yourself and hold yourself together until things get better.

This is how it works. One day, it's midnight and you're in the arms of this person who loves you so much that everything feels unreal around them. Time passes, and that person becomes a memory. You no longer remember the fondness with which they held you, but the way it all ended and how you've been feeling that all your midnights are empty without them. The hurt is easier to remember than the moments that made us feel alive because we fall in love with time, but the hurt mostly comes unexpectedly.

Like a rainbow without colours
that's a human heart without dreams.

Pain has a habit
of making its home
in the hearts of those
who hurt others.

—*Karma*

Learn from your past
instead of trying to forget it.
Moving on is about
accepting and learning,
not ignoring and forgetting.

By hating others,
you're hurting your own heart.

Sometimes when someone's leaving, that's when we realize how much they mean to us. Every moment spent with them flashes before our eyes, and all we want to do is relive every single one of them. All those conversations and silences, all those times they made you laugh and shared your pain, and everything in between. You miss all of it, but it's too late to stop them from leaving. So, while someone is there in your life, while you can hold their hands and hug them, while you can look into their eyes and see love dancing in their irises, take time out to tell them how much you appreciate their presence. Tell them how much they mean to you and how your life wouldn't be the same without them being in it. Tell them how much you adore every little thing they do for you. Tell them how much you value the efforts they make for you. And love them. Love them as much as you can, and never let them go.

The feelings that suffocate your heart,
also give life to your heart.

I hope you find fireflies to give you hope every time you feel lost in the darkness. A shooting star to guide you through every hard night. Sunflowers to fill you with a light on days when negativity surrounds you. And on days when you find no light around you, I hope you remind yourself of the magic that lives in your heart and choose to be your own glimmer of hope.

Your soul deserves a love
that is serene
like the sunset-sky,
a love that feels
like fresh flowers,
old songs
and poetry.

My heart wants me
to dive into oceans
and shoot for the stars.

It wants me
to paint rainbows on the moon
and be my own silver lining.
To sit in silence
and listen to the voice
I've been running away
from forever.

My heart wants me to take risks;
it wants me to feel what
I'm scared of feeling;
it wants me to give life another chance;
it wants me to fall in love again.

Just like a sunset
happiness is
eternally beautiful
but short-lived.

Do you mend your broken heart by giving the pieces to someone else? Or do you love yourself enough to mend it on your own? You read a thousand self-love quotes but are terrified of being alone. That's your problem.

Have faith in the
power of kindness—
rivers stop flowing,
mountains reduce to dust
and hearts melt in no time.

My heart looks at everyone with overflowing compassion and believes they too shelter kindness in their souls. I have been hurt, but my heart doesn't let me hurt others, not even the ones who are responsible for my pain. And I guess everyone has a heart like that, and everyone's capable of kindness and forgiveness. But, sadly, most people don't let their hearts guide them. It's sad that people suppress the voice of their conscience and don't feel bad when they mistreat others. To be kind in a world that has forgotten its roots and values is an act of valiance, and I hope more people will choose to be brave instead of being someone who hates and hurts others.

—*kindness and forgiveness*

Love isn't only about expectations; it's also about acceptance. And most people suffer in love because they fail to acknowledge this.

Filling your mother's heart with joy
is not a favour you do to her,
it's a duty you must
take pride in fulfilling.

You keep trying to
make everyone in your
world happy,
but forget to put a smile
on the faces of the ones
who brought you
into the world.

Sometimes family is just
pieces of a puzzle
scattered around a house,
hopelessly waiting for someone
to put them all back together
and make a home again.

Let love take
all the space in your heart;
let there be no room
for hatred left inside you.

Some hearts speak the
language of love so fluently
that even the ones
who claim to not believe in love
unfurl in front of them
the way flowers do
after a shower of rain.

Love takes people's hearts
in its hands
and turns them into rainbows,
and the hate that they had been
carrying inside them
for so long
gently slips away.

Love will make your heart both, the sky and the storm.

My heart is not a garden
where you can plant love
only to eventually walk away.

I'm not a summer house
you can enter and leave
at convenience.
I'm not a shade for travellers
to rest under.

My heart only
lets someone enter it
when they carry
love in their heart,
respect in their eyes
and warmth in their actions.

This heart is only for those
who genuinely feel like home.

Beautiful are the hearts that are kind to others.

You were a city I fell in love with. I loved you, but you could never feel like *home* to me.

The day you said you loved me,
the sparrows sang soulful songs,
the sun smiled in joy
and the clouds blushed away.

The flowers told me that together,
we made a beautiful poem,
and the sky smiled back.

Love:

- Rainy afternoons, when nature is intoxicated with the fragrance of flowers.
- Sparrows chirping in delight.
- My mother feeding stray dogs. The dogs have a soul. I can feel it every time they dance in joy, looking at her.
- Kids waiting for the ice-cream man and running towards him the moment they see him.
- The stars talking to the moon and the moon ignoring them all. For despite being surrounded by so many stars, the moon is in love with solitude.
- Reading poems in people's eyes.
- Reading poets who write about things other than love.

You took the autumn out of my soul,
that's why I fell for you.

Your name can
freeze flowing rivers,
make stars fall to the ground,
give hope to broken hearts
and set mine on fire.

You entered my life
and it felt like
the end of a brutal war,
and the start of an era of soulful music.

You say there will come a time when I won't love you any more. And I wonder if the flowers can ever stop loving the sun. If the trees can ever stop loving spring. If the rain can ever stop loving the earth. But I don't tell you that. I don't tell you that I will hold on to your memories if you don't hold my hand. That even if someday, I am left with no choice but to walk away, I will leave my heart behind. And if you leave, I will call your name in empty rooms, search for you in every raindrop and never stop waiting for you to come back. I don't tell you that you may leave me, but my love for you won't leave my heart. But what I do tell you is that these feelings are storms. I tell you that these feelings may leave my heart someday, but they will leave me destroyed.

I wish to be someone's favorite poem—
the one that feels like home to them
and always stays in their heart,
the one that gives them strength
when nothing seems to make sense,
the one that holds them gently
on days when the world seems
to be pushing them away.
I wish to be that poem for someone.

Expectations and selfishness complicate things. Love simplifies them.

I don't sing while making my morning coffee. I wake up to the sounds of the rain, and I shut the windows. I plug-in earphones instead of having conversations. I laugh when someone tells me that they love me. I skip meals, love songs and messages. If you're reading this, I hope you won't let this happen to you. Staying with someone for a long time shouldn't end with you forgetting how to be happy alone. Don't stop doing the things you love the most just because the person you loved the most isn't in love with you any more.

Share your light with those hearts
who feel they don't deserve to be loved.

Life is too short
to stay with someone
who kills your peace.

I no longer feel guilty
about putting myself first,
because I'm tired of
giving my best to the people
who leave me alone at my worst.

The worst part is that
I want you to stay,
but don't know
how to stop you
from leaving.

Stay with the one
who has seen both,
the stars in your eyes
and the storms in your heart,
and loved you regardless.

If they keep walking away and coming back,
you must close the door on them forever.

Some people do not believe in magic, and some people are magic themselves. They burn like candles to give light even to the ones who forget to thank them for it. They fill the hearts of others even on days when they themselves feel empty on the inside. They feel like the sun to people, giving light to their souls. Such people are rare and precious, and their kind hearts are a blessing to this world. So, when you find someone like that, someone so selfless and kind, I hope you choose to be a little kinder to them than you usually are to people. I hope you take their hands in your own and thank them with your whole heart. I hope your kindness gives them a reason to continue being kind to others.

When things don't feel right, just keep walking. You'll cross those rivers and climb all those mountains. Fall but never forget that you deserve to fly. Your heart deserves to bloom, not break. Even the most beautiful stories have some bad chapters in them, and that's okay.

You deserve to watch the most beautiful sunsets with someone who has the most beautiful heart. You deserve to laugh until your stomach hurts and your cheeks turn pink. You deserve to dance in joy and be loved in all the seasons. You, my friend, deserve the best things in the world, and may you never let anyone tell you otherwise.

Scan QR code to access the
Penguin Random House India website